Is There More to Life Than This?

C000050253

Booklets taken from Questions of Life:

Is There More to Life Than This?

Who Is Jesus?

Why Did Jesus Die?

How Can We Have Faith?

Why and How Do I Pray?

Why and How Should I Read the Bible?

How Does God Guide Us?

The Holy Spirit

How Can I Resist Evil?

Why and How Should I Tell Others?

Does God Heal Today?

What About the Church?

How Can I Make the Most of the Rest of My Life?

Is There More to Life Than This?

NICKY GUMBEL

Scripture quotations taken from
the Holy Bible, New International
Version Anglicised. Copyright ©
1979, 1984, 2011 Biblica, formerly
International Bible Society. Used by
permission of Hodder & Stoughton
Publishers, an Hachette UK
company. All rights reserved. 'NIV'
is a registered trademark of Biblica.
UK trademark number 1448790.

Published by Alpha International
Holy Trinity Brompton
Brompton Road
London SW7 1JA
Email: publications@alpha.org

Illustrated by Charlie Mackesy

Contents

Is There More to Life Than This?

"LOCHNESS or NOTHINGNESS today Gerald?"

For many years I had three objections to the Christian faith. First, I thought it was boring. I went to chapel at school and found it very dull. I had sympathy with the novelist Robert Louis Stevenson who once entered in his diary, as if recording an extraordinary phenomenon, 'I have been to church today, and am not depressed.' My impression of the Christian faith was that it was dreary and uninspiring.

Second, it seemed to me to be untrue. I had intellectual objections to the Christian faith and described myself as an atheist. In fact, I rather pretentiously called myself a logical determinist. When I was fourteen, I wrote an essay for Religious Studies in which I tried to destroy the whole of Christianity and disprove the existence of God. Rather surprisingly, it was put forward for a prize! I had knock-down arguments against the Christian faith and rather enjoyed arguing with Christians, on each occasion thinking I had won some great victory.

Third, I thought that Christianity was irrelevant to my life. I could not see how something that happened 2,000 years ago and 2,000 miles away in the Middle East could have any relevance to my life today. At school we often used to sing that much-loved hymn 'Jerusalem', which asks, 'And did those feet in ancient time walk upon England's mountains green?' We all knew that the answer was, 'No, they did not.' Jesus never came anywhere near England!

With hindsight, I realise that it was partly my fault as I never really listened and so did not know very much about the Christian faith. There are many people today who don't know much about Jesus Christ, or what he did, or anything else about Christianity.

One hospital chaplain listed some of the replies he was given to the question, 'Would you like Holy Communion?' These are some of the answers:

'No thanks, I'm Church of England.'

'No thanks, I asked for cornflakes.'

'No thanks, I've never been circumcised.'[1]

Not only was I ignorant about the Christian faith but also, looking back, my experience was that something was missing.

In his book *The Audacity of Hope*, President Barack Obama, commenting on his own conversion to Christianity, writes of the hunger in every human heart:

> Each day, it seems, thousands of Americans are going about their daily rounds – dropping off the kids at school, driving to the office, flying to a business meeting, shopping at the mall, trying to stay on their diets – and coming to the realization that something is missing. They are deciding that their work, their possessions, their diversions, their sheer busyness are not enough. They want a sense of purpose, a narrative arc to their lives, something that will relieve a chronic loneliness or lift them above the exhausting, relentless toll of daily life.

> They need an assurance that somebody out there cares about them, is listening to them – that they are not just destined to travel down a long highway toward nothingness.[2]

Men and women were created to live in a relationship with God. Without that relationship there will always be a hunger, an emptiness, a feeling that something is missing. Bernard Levin, perhaps the greatest columnist of his generation, once wrote an article called 'Life's Great Riddle, and No Time to Find its Meaning'. In it he said that in spite of his great success he feared he might have 'wasted reality in the chase of a dream'.

> To put it bluntly, have I time to discover why I was born before I die?... I have not managed to answer the question yet, and however many years I have before me they are certainly not as many as there are behind. There is an obvious danger in leaving it too late... why do I *have* to know why I was born? Because, of course, I am unable to believe that it was an accident; and if it wasn't one, it must have a meaning.[3]

He was not religious, writing on one occasion, 'For the fourteen thousandth time, I am not a Christian.' Yet he seemed only too aware of the inadequate answers to the meaning of life. He wrote some years earlier:

Countries like ours are full of people who have all the material comforts they desire, together with such non-material blessings as a happy family, and yet lead lives of quiet, and at times noisy, desperation, understanding nothing but the fact that there is a hole inside them and that however much food and drink they pour into it, however many motor cars and television sets they stuff it with, however many well-balanced children and loyal friends they parade around the edges of it... it aches.[4]

Jesus Christ said, 'I am the way and the truth and the life' (John 14:6). The implications of his claim were as startling in the first century as they are in the twenty-first. So what are we to make of it?

Direction for a lost world

First, Jesus said, 'I am the way'. When their children were younger, some friends of mine had a Swedish nanny. She was struggling to learn the English language, and still hadn't quite mastered all the English idioms. On one occasion, an argument broke out between the children in their bedroom. The nanny rushed upstairs to sort it out, and what she meant to say was, 'What on earth are you doing?' What she actually said was, 'What are you doing on earth?' This is a very good question, 'What are we doing on earth?'

In 1879, Leo Tolstoy, author of *War and Peace* and *Anna Karenina*, wrote a book called *A Confession*, in which he tells the story of his search for meaning and purpose in life. He had rejected Christianity as a child. When he left university he sought to get as much pleasure out of life as he could. He threw himself into the social worlds of Moscow and St Petersburg, drinking heavily, sleeping around, gambling and leading a wild life. But he found it did not satisfy him.

Then he became ambitious for money. He had inherited an estate and made a large amount of money out of his books. Yet that did not satisfy him either. He sought success, fame and importance. These he also achieved. He wrote what the *Encyclopaedia Britannica* describes as 'one of the two or three greatest novels in world literature'. But he was left asking the question, 'Well fine... so what?', to which he had no answer.

Then he became ambitious for his family – to give them the best possible life. He married in 1862 and had a kind, loving wife and thirteen children (which, he said, distracted him from any search for the overall meaning of life!). He had achieved all his ambitions and was surrounded by what appeared to be complete happiness. And yet one question brought him to the verge of suicide: 'Is there any meaning in my life which will not be annihilated by the inevitability of death which awaits me?'

He searched for the answer in every field of science and philosophy. The only answer he could find to the question, 'Why do I live?' was that 'in the infinity of space and the infinity of time infinitely small particles mutate with infinite complexity.' Not finding that answer hugely satisfying, he looked round at his contemporaries and found that many of them were simply avoiding the issue. Eventually he found among Russia's peasants the answer he had been looking for: their faith in Jesus Christ. He wrote after his conversion that he was 'led inescapably by experience to the conviction that only... faith give[s] life a meaning'.[5]

Over 100 years later, nothing has changed. Freddie Mercury, the lead singer of the rock group Queen, who died at the end of 1991, wrote in one of his last songs on *The Miracle* album, 'Does anybody know what we are living for?' In spite of the fact that he had amassed a huge fortune and had attracted thousands of fans, he admitted in an interview shortly before his death that he was desperately lonely. He said, 'You can have everything in the world and still be the loneliest man, and that is the most bitter type of loneliness. Success has brought me world idolisation and millions of pounds, but it's prevented me from having the one thing we all need – a loving, ongoing relationship.'

Freddie Mercury was right to speak of an 'ongoing relationship' as the one thing we all need. Ultimately there is only one relationship that is completely loving and totally ongoing: a relationship with God. Jesus said, 'I am the way'. He is the only One who can bring us into that relationship with God that goes on into eternity.

When I was a child our family had an old black and white television set. We could never get a very good picture: on one occasion, during the World Cup final in 1966, just as England were about to score a goal, the screen went fuzzy, disintegrating into lines. We were quite happy with it since we did not know anything different. We tried to improve the picture by treading on certain floorboards and standing in certain places near it. Then we discovered that what the television needed was an outside aerial! Suddenly we could get clear and distinct pictures. Our enjoyment was transformed. Life without a relationship with Jesus Christ is like the television without the aerial. Some people seem quite happy, because they don't realise that there is something better. Once we have experienced a relationship with God, the purpose and meaning of life become clearer. We see things that we have never seen and we understand why we were made.

Reality in a confused world

Second, Jesus said, 'I am the truth'. Sometimes people say, 'It does not matter what you believe so long as you are sincere.' But it is possible to be sincerely wrong. Adolf Hitler was sincerely wrong. His beliefs destroyed the lives of millions of people. The Yorkshire Ripper believed that he was doing God's will when he killed prostitutes. He too was sincerely wrong. His beliefs affected his behaviour. These are extreme examples, but they make the point that it matters a great deal what we believe, because what we believe will dictate how we live.

Other people's response to a Christian may be, 'It's great for you, but it is not for me.' This is not a logical position. If Christianity is true, it is of vital importance to every one of us. If it is not true, it is not 'great for us' – it is very sad, and it means that Christians are deluded. As the writer and scholar C. S. Lewis put it, 'Christianity is a statement which, if false, is of no importance, and, if true, of infinite importance. The one thing it cannot be is moderately important.'[6]

Is it true? Is there any evidence to support Jesus' claim to be 'the truth'? These are some of the questions we will be looking at later in this book. The linchpin of Christianity is the resurrection of Jesus Christ from the dead and for that there is ample evidence, which we will look at in the following booklet.

I don't think I ever realised how much the course of history has been shaped by people who believed that Jesus really was 'the truth'. Lord Denning, widely thought of as one of the greatest legal minds in the twentieth century, was for nearly forty years president of the Lawyers' Christian Fellowship. He had applied his legendary powers of analysis to the historical evidence for Jesus' birth, death and resurrection and concluded that Christianity was true.

I had not appreciated either that some of the most sophisticated philosophers the West has ever produced – Aquinas, Descartes, Locke, Pascal, Leibniz, Kant – were all committed Christians. In fact, two of the most influential philosophers living today, Charles Taylor and Alasdair MacIntyre, have both built a great deal of their work on a deep commitment to Jesus Christ.

Nor had I realised how many of the pioneers of modern science were Christian believers: Galileo, Copernicus, Kepler, Newton, Mendel, Pasteur and Maxwell. This is still true of leading scientists today. Francis Collins, director of the Human Genome Project and one of the most respected geneticists in the world, tells of a mountain walk during which he was so overwhelmed by the beauty of creation that, in his words, 'I knelt in the dewy grass as the sun rose and surrendered to Jesus Christ.'[7]

These words highlight the fact that when Jesus said, 'I am the truth,' he meant more than just intellectual truth. He meant a personal knowledge of someone who fully embodies that truth. The Hebrew understanding of truth is one of experienced reality. It's the difference between knowing something in your head and knowing it in your heart.

Suppose that before I met my wife Pippa I had read a book about her. Then, after I had finished reading the book I thought, 'She sounds like an amazing woman. This is the person I want to marry.' There would be a big difference in my state of mind then – intellectually convinced that she was a wonderful person – and my state of mind now after the experience of many years of marriage from which I can say, 'I know she is a wonderful person.' When a Christian says, in relation to their faith, 'I know Jesus is the truth,' they do not mean only that they know intellectually that he is the truth, but that they have experienced Jesus as the truth.

Life in a dark world

Third, Jesus said, 'I am the life'. The Christian view has always been that people are made in the image of God. As a result there is something noble about every human being. This conviction has been the driving force behind many of the great social reformers, from William Wilberforce to Martin Luther King Jr and Desmond Tutu. But there is also another side to the coin.

Alexander Solzhenitsyn, a Russian writer who won the Nobel Prize for Literature and was converted to

Christianity when in exile from the Soviet Union, said, 'The line separating good and evil passes, not through states, nor through classes, nor between political parties... but right through every human heart and through all human hearts.'[8]

I used to think I was a 'nice' person – because I didn't rob banks or commit other serious crimes. Only when I began to see my life alongside the life of Jesus Christ did I realise how much was wrong.

We all need forgiveness and it can only be found in Christ. Marghanita Laski, a humanist, made an amazing confession during a TV debate with a Christian. She said, 'What I envy about you Christians is your forgiveness.' Then she added rather wistfully, 'I have no one to forgive me.'[9]

What Jesus did when he was crucified for us was to pay the penalty for all the things that we have done wrong. We will look at this subject in more detail in the booklet, *Why Did Jesus Die?*. There, we will see that he died to remove our guilt and to set us free from addictions, fear and death.

Jesus not only died for us, he was also raised from the dead for us. In this act he defeated death. Jesus came to bring us 'eternal life'. Eternal life is a quality of life which comes from living in a relationship with God (John 17:3). Jesus never promised anyone an easy life, but he promised fullness of life (John 10:10).

Alice Cooper, the veteran rock musician, once gave an interview to *The Sunday Times* headlined: 'Alice Cooper has a dark secret – the 53-year-old rocker is a Christian.' In this interview, he describes his conversion to Christianity. 'It hasn't been easy combining religion and rock. It's the most rebellious thing I've ever done. Drinking beer is easy. Trashing your hotel room is easy. But being a Christian, that's a tough call. That's real rebellion.'[10]

The theologian and philosopher Paul Tillich described the human condition as one that always involves three fears: fear of guilt, fear of meaninglessness, and fear of death. Jesus Christ meets each of these fears head on, because he is 'the way and the truth and the life'.[11]

" .. and fear of life without Chocolate "

Endnotes

1. Ronald Brown (ed), *Bishop's Brew* (Arthur James Ltd, 1989).

2. Barack Obama, *The Audacity of Hope: Thoughts on Reclaiming the American Dream* (Canongate Books Ltd, 2008), p.202.

3. By kind permission of Bernard Levin.

4. *Ibid.*

5. Leo Tolstoy, *A Confession and Other Religious Writings* (Penguin, 1988).

6. C. S. Lewis, *'Timeless at Heart'* in *Christian Apologetics* (Fount, 2000).

7. Francis Collins, *The Language of God* (Free Press, 2006).

8. Alexander Solzhenitsyn, *The Gulag Archipelago, 1918–1956: An Experiment in Literary Investigation*, Vol. I (Basic Books, 1997).

9. Quoted by Philip Yancey, *What's So Amazing About Grace?* (Zondervan, 1997), p.279.

10. *The Sunday Times*, 22 September 2001.

11. Paul Tillich, *Writings on Religion*, ed Robert P. Scharlemann (Walter de Gruyter, 1987), p.160.

Alpha

Alpha is a practical introduction to the Christian faith, initiated by HTB in London and now being run by thousands of churches, of many denominations, throughout the world. If you are interested in finding out more about the Christian faith and would like details of your nearest Alpha, please visit our website:

alpha.org

or contact:
The Alpha Office,
HTB Brompton Road,
London,
SW7 1JA

Tel: 0845 644 7544

Alpha titles available

Why Jesus? A booklet – given to all participants at the start of Alpha. 'The clearest, best illustrated and most challenging short presentation of Jesus that I know.' – Michael Green

Why Christmas? The Christmas version of *Why Jesus?*

Questions of Life Alpha in book form. In fifteen compelling chapters Nicky Gumbel points the way to an authentic Christianity which is exciting and relevant to today's world.

Searching Issues The seven issues most often raised by participants on Alpha, including, suffering, other religions, science and Christianity, and the Trinity.

A Life Worth Living What happens after Alpha? Based on the book of Philippians, this is an invaluable next step for those who have just completed Alpha, and for anyone eager to put their faith on a firm biblical footing.

The Jesus Lifestyle   Studies in the Sermon on the Mount showing how Jesus' teaching flies in the face of a modern lifestyle and presents us with a radical alternative.

30 Days   Nicky Gumbel selects thirty passages from the Old and New Testament which can be read over thirty days. It is designed for those on Alpha and others who are interested in beginning to explore the Bible.

All titles are by Nicky Gumbel,
who is vicar of Holy Trinity Brompton

About the Author

Nicky Gumbel is the pioneer of Alpha. He read law at Cambridge and theology at Oxford, practised as a barrister and is now vicar of HTB in London. He is the author of many bestselling books about the Christian faith, including *Questions of Life*, *The Jesus Lifestyle*, *Why Jesus?*, *A Life Worth Living*, *Searching Issues* and *30 Days*.